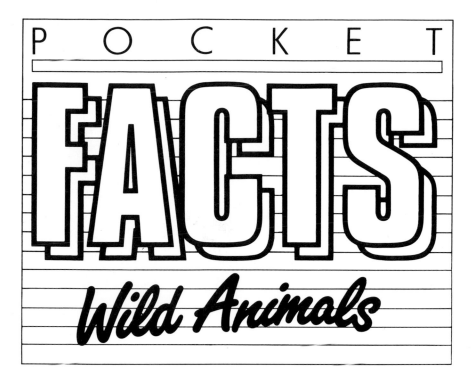

POCKET

FACTS

Wild Animals

Philip Steele

MACMILLAN

Prehistoric animals

The story of today's wild animals stretches back far into the past. The ancestors of today's bears and tigers roamed the Earth millions of years ago.

We can find out about prehistoric animals by studying their fossils. Long ago, the dead bodies of animals became covered by mud. Their remains, or the marks they left behind, slowly hardened and turned into stone. Fossils show us that new kinds of animals began to develop on Earth about 200 million years ago. We call them mammals.

Discovery! A dinosaur's footprint (above). The first mammals appeared on Earth as the dinosaurs were dying out.

Fossils tell us how animals have developed over the ages.

Why do species die out?

Fossil remains tell us that many types, or species, of animals have changed over the ages. The world itself keeps changing. Over millions of years, seas have come and gone, steamy forests have given way to icy glaciers. If animals cannot adapt, they die out.

In recent years people have quickened this process of change. Hunters use guns instead of spears. Machines are used to clear forests.

The quagga was a relative of the zebra. It lived in the grasslands of Africa. Farmers wanted to graze their cattle there, so they hunted the quagga until none were left.

quagga

The secrets of survival

If you look at the bodies of wild animals, you will see that each species has found its own way of surviving. Some have developed sharp teeth for tearing flesh. Others have spines to protect them from attack, or thick fur to keep out the cold. The body of the armadillo on the left is protected against attack by nine bands of bony armour. It has a long tongue for eating insects, and sharp claws for digging. There are 20 species of armadillo. Each has developed its own weapons and skills.

3

What are mammals?

The animals in this book are mammals. This means that the mothers feed their babies milk. Most mammals give birth to live young. Only two kinds of mammal, the echidnas and the duck-billed platypus, lay eggs.

There are 4230 mammal species, including cats and dogs, mice and bats, elephants and giraffes, monkeys and apes – and humans. Scientists have divided mammals into groups that look alike. The cheetah belongs to the cat family, and the wolf to the dog family. Most mammals are land dwellers, but some have learned to fly and others have learned to swim. Most mammals are covered in hair or fur. Some have a thick hide. Mammals are the most intelligent of all creatures.

bonnet monkey feeding young

Heavy sleepers

Mammals are warm-blooded creatures. This means that, unlike reptiles, their bodies make their own heat. Energy is provided by the food they eat. In winter food can be scarce, so some mammals, like this dormouse (left) save energy by sleeping through the whole winter. Its heartbeat slows down and its temperature drops. This is called hibernation.

How mammals keep warm

polar bear

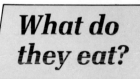

The mammals' central heating system is helped by the hair, wool or fur with which most of them are covered. This coat traps cold air and warms it. Some mammals have waterproof fur to protect them from the damp.

Mammals also have a layer of fat in their bodies to keep in the warmth. Some mammals that live in icy seas feed their young with very fatty milk. This helps them grow an extra thick layer of fat or blubber.

elephant seals

tiger

What do they eat?

All mammals need to eat food for energy. Many, such as zebra, eat only plants. We call them herbivores. Others, such as tigers, eat the flesh of other animals. Tigers hunt deer, pigs and buffalo. We call them carnivores. Some animals, like humans, will eat both plants and animals. We call them omnivores.

5

What are marsupials?

Most mammals have already developed into smaller versions of their parents by the time they are born. They have grown inside their mothers, fed by a rich supply of blood.

However some mammal babies are not fully formed at birth. They are not ready to go out into the world so they crawl into a pouch on the mother's belly. Here they can drink milk, and stay warm and safe. They do not leave the pouch until they can fend for themselves.

Pouched mammals are known as marsupials. Kangaroos, wallabies, koalas, bandicoots and opossums are all marsupials.

koalas

Where do they live?

Once upon a time, marsupials were found in many parts of the world. Over millions of years most species died out, but in Australia many survived. In South America too the opossums survived, later crossing to North America.

There are about 250 marsupial species alive today. Many of them look like more common mammals. There are marsupial versions of moles, squirrels and mice. The largest marsupial is the red kangaroo (above). The smallest is the mouse-sized Kimberley planigale. One of the best-known marsupials is the koala (left), which lives in the gum trees of Australia.

The upside-down sloth

three-toed sloth

The sloth is not a marsupial, but it is a very strange creature. It spends a lot of its life hanging upside-down from trees in the rain forests of South America. Its long, hooked claws help it to hang on tight. Its shaggy coat sometimes becomes so damp that algae grow on it. These tiny plants can make the sloth look green!

The sloth is a shambling, slow creature. It feeds on leaves, shoots and forest fruits, and can turn its head far round without moving its body. The sloth spends much of the day asleep, propped in the fork of a tree. Its main enemies are eagles, snakes, and big cats such as the jaguar.

Termites for dinner

giant anteater

Anteaters break open the nests of termites and ants with their claws and eat the insects with their long, sticky tongues.

7

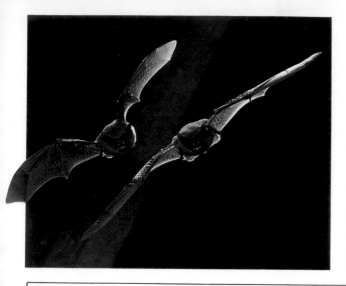

How do bats fly?

There are about 800 species of bat. They are the only mammals that can really fly. Their body skin is stretched over bony arms, fingers, and legs to form leathery wings. In some species the wings also join the legs to the tail. Bats move their limbs to and fro in order to fly. Some species carry their babies in flight.

How do bats hunt?

Bats have poor eye-sight. They use sound to hunt their prey and to avoid obstacles. As bats fly they give out rapid, very high-pitched squeaks. Humans can only hear the lowest of these notes. The waves of sound bounce off objects. These echoes guide the bats through the air.

horseshoe bat

echoes return

moth

waves of sound

Why is a hedgehog spiny?

The body of an adult hedgehog is covered in up to 7000 stiff spines. When hedgehogs are under attack they roll up into a tight ball. The spines protect the hedgehog's soft belly. Each spine is made of hollow, rigid sections of hair. There are 17 hedgehog species found in Asia, Europe and Africa. They eat slugs, snails, beetles, lizards and snakes. They are hunted in turn by badgers and foxes. The spines of the hedgehog protect it well against its traditional enemies, but are of little use against more modern hazards. Thousands of hedgehogs are run over by cars each year.

rolled up against attack

walking

Can moles see?

Some mammals have adapted to a life underground. The mole has strong forelegs and claws for digging tunnels.
It has little need for good eyesight, as it hunts in the darkness. Its tiny eyes are hidden in the fur of its black velvet snout. They cannot see objects clearly, but can tell the difference between dark and light. To make up for poor sight, moles have a good sense of smell, hearing and touch. These help moles in their endless search for tasty earthworms.

What are rodents?

harvest mouse

The word rodent means 'gnawing', and that is what this group of mammals does best. All rodents have powerful front teeth. Rats and mice are the most common rodents. Mice mostly eat seeds and grain. Rats will eat almost anything. They have become a serious pest for humans, as they eat our food and spread disease. The harvest mouse is Europe's smallest rodent. It lives in fields of wheat and in hedgerows.

Saving for winter

red squirrel

Tree squirrels are a type of rodent. They scramble along branches and leap from tree to tree. Their treetop nests are known as 'dreys'. Squirrels like to eat nuts and acorns. When autumn comes they hide away stores of food for the cold winter months. Red squirrels are found through much of Europe and Asia. They are often found in evergreen woods, where they gnaw fir cones for the seeds.

Animal engineers

Beavers feed on bark and saplings. Their large front teeth serve as hatchets. These swimming rodents are expert lumberjacks. They can gnaw their way through whole tree trunks, to dam rivers, and build lodges where they can live.

lodge

North American beaver

dam

Cottontail racers

brown hare

Rabbits and hares are not rodents, but they too have large front teeth, which they use to nibble grass and shoots.
Hares are larger than rabbits, and live in the open. They have strong back legs and can escape from danger at a speed of 65 kilometres per hour.

Stoats and weasels

Stoats and weasels and their relatives belong to a group of mammals called mustelids. The group includes otters, badgers, wolverines, skunks, polecats and many others. There are 67 species. Some stoats and weasels in cold regions have a white coat in winter, to avoid being seen in the snow. Most mustelids have long, lithe bodies and short legs. Badgers and wolverines are larger, with powerful, stocky bodies.

stoat

least weasel

The stoat is a fierce hunter of rabbits. It can swim, climb and slip through the undergrowth with ease. Weasels are smaller, but are also fierce. They hunt rodents. The least weasel of North America is the smallest carnivore, with a body about 10cm long.

Along the river bank

giant otter

Some mustelids are expert swimmers. Mink will hunt frogs and fish, and so will otters. Otters have webbed feet and waterproof fur. Some otter species live in rivers, lakes and marshes. Some live in the sea.

European mink

Why do skunks smell?

Mustelids are famous stinkers! They give out a strong, musky smell. Many of them, such as the polecat, use this scent to mark out the area where they live. It warns rivals to keep away from the territory. Skunks live in North America. They use their stench glands to scare off attackers. They can squirt stinking juice over 3.5 metres! The skunk's stripes act as a warning to keep clear.

polecat

skunk

Claws for digging

Badgers are among the larger mustelids. They have long claws for digging out their underground dens, or setts. The European badger has a black-and-white face and a grizzled coat. The American badger is similar but smaller. Badgers eat worms, snails, insects, mice, hedgehogs and plants.

European badger

Night scavengers

The raccoon lives in North and Central America. It is a bear-like mammal about the size of a pet cat, with a bushy, black-ringed tail. It has a black 'mask' around the eyes, which makes it look like a bank robber. Raccoons sneak into farms by night and steal eggs, grain and rubbish. They also feed on worms and insects, and search through shallow streams for shellfish, frogs and fish.

raccoon

The pandas

The pandas were once thought to be relatives of the bears, but scientists today think that they are more like raccoons. The lesser or red panda certainly looks like a large raccoon, with thick red fur and a bushy tail. The giant panda is 20 times heavier and more like a cuddly bear. It has black and white markings.

lesser or red panda

Why are pandas at risk?

The pandas live in the mountains and forests of Tibet and Sichuan, in south west China. They feed on bamboo shoots, grass, roots, small birds and mammals. The forests where they live are being cleared, and today only 500 or so giant pandas survive in the wild. They are strictly protected by law, for they are difficult to breed in captivity. Red pandas are also rare, but can be bred more easily.

giant panda

The brown bear

brown bear

Brown bears are found in North America and Europe. The biggest are found on Kodiak Island, off Alaska. Males have been known to weigh 75 kilogrammes.

polar bear

The Arctic hunter

The huge polar bear has white fur to hide it against the snow and ice. It eats seals, fish, birds, berries and plants, and will attack humans. It is a strong swimmer.

15

The cunning of the fox

red fox
earth

The dog family is well known to humans, as we first tamed dogs about 12 000 years ago. If tame dogs have been our best friends, their wild relatives have been treated as our worst enemies. These include wolves, foxes, jackals, and dingoes.

There are nine species of fox. The red fox (left) is famed for its cunning. It lives in North America, Africa, Asia and Europe, and eats snails, small mammals, birds and insects. It raids farms and city dustbins. Red foxes live in a den called an earth. The cubs are born in the spring. A male fox is called a dog, and the female is called a vixen. Foxes have been hunted and killed by farmers for centuries, but still survive.

Living in the desert

The smallest fox is the fennec, (left) which lives in the deserts of North Africa and the Middle East. Its huge ears help its body to lose heat, and it can survive without water for days on end. Its soft, cream-coloured coat also helps to keep off the rays of the sun. The fennec only weighs about 1.5 kg. During the heat of the day the fennec often hides in burrows. At night it comes out to hunt, eating lizards and snakes, spiders and scorpions, and the smallest desert mammals.

The coyote is like a small wolf. It lives in North America and hunts birds and small mammals. Coyote hunt as a pack, in pairs, or singly. They will sometimes raid city rubbish tips.

The dog family signal to each other with their bodies.

This coyote signals fear by putting his tail between his legs.

The leader of the coyote pack bares his teeth. This is a sign of aggression.

Running wild

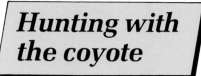

dingo

Wild dogs can be vicious hunters. The Cape hunting dog lives on the plains of Africa. The pack hunts together, running down zebra and buffalo. Dingoes are wild dogs found in the Australian outback. They hunt in small packs and attack kangaroos, as well as sheep and poultry. They are often hunted by farmers protecting their livestock. The first dingoes probably came to Australia in prehistoric times, as tame hunting dogs. Later, they ran wild.

17

The biggest cat of all

The cat family takes in lions, tigers, and leopards as well as your own pet kitten. The biggest cat of all is the magnificent tiger (right) which lives in the jungles of Asia. A male can weigh over 230 kg. Tigers normally hunt on their own at night, and spend the day in a shady spot in the jungle.

A plan of attack

Most lions live in Africa. The females do much of the hunting. Some will slip behind a herd of zebra or wildebeeste and make them panic. They then drive them straight into an ambush. A victim is singled out and dragged down.

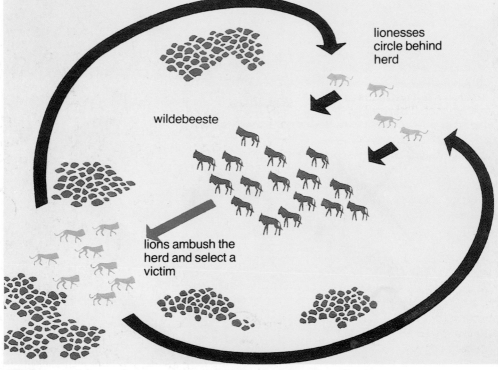

lionesses circle behind herd

wildebeeste

lions ambush the herd and select a victim

cheetah

The sprint champion

The world's fastest land animal is the cheetah. It is a long, lithe cat with a body built for speed. It is said to be able to reach nearly 100 kph over short distances. Cheetahs live in Africa and the Middle East, where they were once captured and trained to hunt. In the wild they hunt antelope, ostriches and small mammals. Cheetahs do not hunt their prey by stalking and ambush. They simply put on a burst of speed, exhaust the victim and run it down.

How do cats stay hidden?

Many mammals have colours that make them hard to see. This is called camouflage. It helps hunters hide from their prey, and it helps the victim avoid being seen.

The leopard (right) has a spotted coat. This makes it hard to see among the leaves and dappled shadows of the African bush. The tiger's stripes work in the same way, blending in with the shadows of grasses and trees in the moonlit jungle. The plain, tawny coat of the lion is the same colour as the grass of the sunbaked, open plains of Africa. Not all animals use their markings to stay hidden. The bold black and white stripes of the zebra are meant to dazzle and confuse the lion as it chases the herd.

What are antlers for?

antlers

for the first seven years, each new set of antlers has more branches than the previous set

red deer stag

Many deer carry a fine pair of branching antlers made of solid bone. These can be used for digging up moss, for scratching backs and for fighting during the mating season. The antlers are shed each year. The new bone grows beneath skin known as velvet.

Safety in the herd

Antelopes like the springboks (left) live in a herd. When they are attacked, they turn and gallop, leaping high into the air. In the confusion, most of the herd escapes. Antelopes are related to goats, sheep and cattle, and many graze the grassy plains of Asia and Africa. Others have adapted to a life in forests, wetlands, deserts or mountains.

Why such a long neck?

The giraffe (right) is the tallest animal in the world. A relative of the antelopes, it has a long, long neck. The male can stand 5.5 metres tall. The giraffe's neck helps it to reach the leaves of tall trees. Its favourite food is the thorny acacia of the African bush. The neck also helps the giraffe to keep a look out for lions lurking behind bushes. Having such a long neck creates some problems. In order to drink from a pool, the giraffe must spread its forelegs wide apart and lower its neck to the water. Fortunately, the giraffe can obtain much of the water it needs from juicy leaves. The giraffe needs an especially powerful heart, in order to pump blood all the way up to the head.

Arabian camel

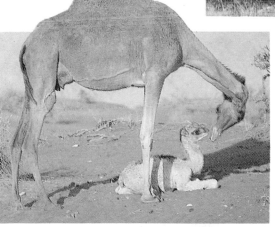

What is the hump for?

There are two species of camel. The Arabian camel or dromedary has one hump. The Bactrian camel has two. Both kinds live in deserts. The fatty humps provide the camel with energy when food is scarce.

A male African elephant weighs about six tonnes and stands 3.5 metres high. It is normally a gentle giant, eating only plants. In the wild it can eat up to 220kg of leaves and drink 100 litres of water in a single day. Food and drink are passed to its mouth by its long trunk, which is also used for smelling and touching. The elephant is so huge that no other animal will attack it. Only humans hunt the elephant, killing it with guns. People hunt it for the ivory of its fine tusks. Today the African elephant is protected within game parks, but many are still shot.

African or Indian?

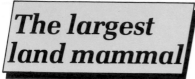

Indian elephant

African elephant

There are two species of elephant living today. The African is the biggest. It has been known to weigh over 10.5 tonnes. Its large, flapping ears help its body to keep cool in the heat. The Indian elephant is smaller. It has a high, domed shape to its head. It lives in shady forests and so has smaller ears. The Indian elephant has been tamed for thousands of years. It can be used for shifting timber in logging camps and often appears in ceremonial parades.

Ancient monsters

Rhinoceroses (below) have been roaming the Earth for about 60 million years. There are five species living today. The black and the white rhinos live in Africa, and the Javan, Sumatran and great Indian rhinos live in Asia. All species are heavyweights. The black rhino can weigh over three tonnes. It has two horns made of compacted fibre on its snout.

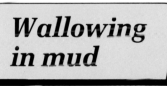

Wallowing in mud

The name hippopotamus means 'river horse', but hippos look more like giant pigs. There are two species. The common hippo (below) lives in African rivers such as the Nile. The rare pygmy hippo lives in the forests of West Africa.

A mountain of blubber

The northern elephant seal is a sea mammal that lives off the coasts of California and Central America. Its southern cousin is found in the icy waters that lie between the Malvinas or Falkland Islands and Antarctica. Both are vast animals which can weigh over 3.5 tonnes. The male, or bull, has a long, floppy nose, from which it gets its name. In the breeding season this helps the bull roar and so attract a mate.

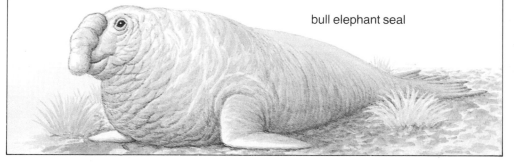

bull elephant seal

What is a true seal?

Sealions and fur seals have ears on the outside of their bodies. The ears of true seals, such as the elephant and monk, cannot be seen.

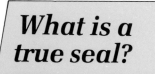

monk seal

True seals and eared seals are all good swimmers. Their rear flippers push them forward through the water. Their fore flippers help them steer. Food includes fish, crabs, shrimps, squid and seabirds. They come ashore to breed in spring, gathering in large numbers on beaches, rocks and icefloes.

sealion

Why do dolphins jump?

Although dolphins look like fish, they are really mammals. Fish can take in life-giving oxygen directly from the water, but whales, porpoises and dolphins have lungs and must breathe in their oxygen from the air. They breathe out through blow-holes in their foreheads. Dolphins and porpoises travel through the water in groups known as schools. They leap high into the air to breathe. Whales too must surface to breathe. The warm air they breathe out forms a great spout of vapour

Squeaks and clicks

Dolphins, porpoises and whales belong to a group of mammals called cetaceans (*set-ay-shuns*). They are among the most intelligent mammals. They signal to each other with squeaks and clicking noises.

Cetaceans can be taught all kinds of skills and many have been tamed. Even wild dolphins seem to enjoy playing with humans, entering bays and allowing bathers to swim with them. Humans have repaid the friendship of these intelligent creatures by slaughtering them. Many cetaceans are in danger of becoming extinct.

Killer whale

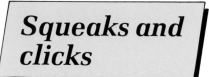

blow-hole

flippers are forelegs
adapted for swimming.

flukes

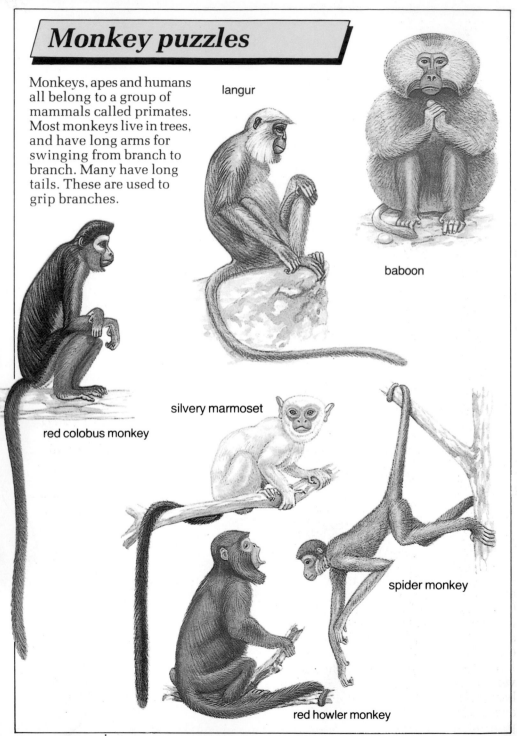

Monkey puzzles

Monkeys, apes and humans all belong to a group of mammals called primates. Most monkeys live in trees, and have long arms for swinging from branch to branch. Many have long tails. These are used to grip branches.

langur

baboon

red colobus monkey

silvery marmoset

spider monkey

red howler monkey

26

The intelligent apes

chimpanzee

Apes look like monkeys, but they have little or no tails. They are able to walk upright and have well-developed brains. Chimpanzees signal to each other with all kinds of gestures. Scientists have studied these and learned to exchange 'messages' with them. Chimps can also use simple tools. Apes are humans' closest relatives in the animal world.

The largest ape

Gibbons and orang-utans are apes that are found in the jungles of Asia. Chimpanzees and gorillas live in African forests. Gorillas are the biggest apes, the average male standing over 1.75m tall. Gorillas are strictly plant-eaters and live in troops led by a male. The male is very powerful. When challenged, it will beat its chest and hoot. This may seem aggressive, but gorillas are really peaceful creatures.

Protecting our wildlife

The world's great wildernesses are vanishing. The prairies of North America are now farmed and settled by people. The bison that grazed them very nearly became extinct, but were saved just in time. All over the world, mammals and other creatures are in danger. Laws must be passed to protect them.

North American bison

How the oryx was saved

The Arabian oryx is an antelope that was once common in the deserts of the Middle East. It was hunted until it was almost extinct. However in the 1960s wild oryx were captured and bred abroad. After some years it was possible to return a number of Arabian oryx to their former home. Many such rescue operations have taken place. Humans will have to change their attitude to their fellow creatures.

The record breakers

★ The biggest animal on Earth is the blue whale, which lives in the Atlantic, Pacific and Indian Oceans. Females of the southern oceans have an average length of 26 metres and weigh 109 tonnes.

★ The biggest land animal is the African elephant. The largest on record was over four metres high and weighed 10.7 tonnes.

★ The tallest animal on record was a 5.9 metre high giraffe.

★ The smallest mammal is Kitti's hog-nosed bat, which lives in Thailand. It has a body length of about three centimetres, and a wing span of about 16 centimetres.

★ The fastest mammal sprinter is the cheetah, which is thought to be able to reach speeds of nearly 100 kph. However, the pronghorn antelope of North America has more stamina and can keep up speeds of about 48 kph for nearly a quarter of an hour.

★ The clumsy sloth is the champion slowcoach of the mammal world. It takes over six hours to travel one kilometre.

★ The mammal that lives to the ripest old age, not counting humans, is the Indian elephant. One was known to have lived for 70 years.

★ The highest-living mammal is the Tibetan wild yak, which will graze mountain plants at altitudes of over 6000 metres.

★ The most aggressive wild animal is said to be the Cape buffalo of Africa. A bull weighs a tonne, and its charge is unstoppable.

★ The most dangerous pest is the rat. It can bite people and cause food poisoning. It can carry deadly fleas which spread bubonic plague. Six hundred years ago the plague killed 25 million people in Europe alone. Rats and their fleas can spread all kinds of other killer diseases.

blue whale

Index

The numbers in **bold** are illustrations.

First published 1990

Published by Macmillan Children's Books
A division of MACMILLAN PUBLISHERS LTD
Houndmills, Basingstoke, Hampshire RG21 2XS
and London
Companies and representatives
throughout the world

Design by Julian Holland Publishing Ltd
Cover concept by Groom and Pickerill

Printed in Hong Kong

British Library Cataloguing in Publication Data

Steele, Philip
  Wild Animals
  1. Animals – For children
  I. Title II. Series
  591

  ISBN 0-333-51453-X

Acknowledgements
Illustrations: BLA Publishing Limited; Martin Smillie
Photographs: *a = above m = middle b = below*
2a ZEFA; 2b P Green/Ardea London; 3b Haroldo Palo Jr/NHPA; 4a Jany Sauvanet/NHPA; 4b and 5a Aquila; 5m Ed Lawrenson; 5b E Hanumantha Rao/NHPA; 6a ZEFA; 6b Douglass Baglin/NHPA; 7a Haroldo Palo Jr/NHPA; 7b Jany Sauvanet/NHPA; 8a Stephen Dalton/NHPA; 8m G Anderson/NHPA; 9b M C Wilkes/Aquila;10a Aquila; 10b G D T /NHPA; 13b Stephen Dalton/NHPA; 14a Philippa Scott/NHPA; 14b John Shaw/NHPA; 15a Philippa Scott/NHPA; 15b left Stephen Krasemann/NHPA; 15b right Wayne Lankinen/Aquila; 16a Wayne Lankinen/Aquila; 16b Peter Johnson/NHPA; 17b Australian Information Service; 18a E Hanumantha Rao/NHPA; 19a M C Wilkes/Aquila; 19b Peter Johnson/NHPA; 20a Manfred Danegger/NHPA; 20b Peter Johnson/NHPA; 21a M C Wilkes/Aquila; 21b ZEFA; 22a, 23a and b M C Wilkes/Aquila; 25a Scott Johnson/NHPA; 27a Michael Leach/NHPA; 27b R Knightbridge/NHPA; 28a Jonathan Scott/Seaphot; 28m Jany Sauvanet/NHPA; 28b Douglas Dickens/NHPA.

32